The Prayers
of
Saint Isaac
of Nineveh

Translated with an Introduction by
Sebastian Brock

SLG Press

Fairacres Publications 216

ISBN 978-0-7283-0386-7
ISSN 0307-1405

Cover illustration: Icon of St Isaac the Syrian by Mary Hansbury (author's collection).

Edited, Designed and Typeset in Palatino Linotype and Quintessential by Julia Craig-McFeely

SLG Press
Convent of the Incarnation
Fairacres • Oxford
www.slgpress.co.uk

Printed by
Grosvenor Group Ltd, Loughton, Essex

CONTENTS

INTRODUCTION

TRANSLATIONS

INTRODUCTION

INTRODUCTION

Who was Isaac?

Our scant knowledge of the life of Isaac the Syrian, or Isaac of Nineveh, is almost entirely based on two brief biographical notices.[1] According to these he originated from the Qatar region where he became a monk. It is known that in the seventh century Beth Qatraye, on the West of the Gulf, was an important intellectual centre for the Church of the East, and the writings of several authors from this region have survived. In 676 the Catholicos of the Church of the East visited Beth Qatraye and took Isaac back with him, making him Bishop of Nineveh (Mosul). After only a few months in office, he resigned 'for reasons only God knows', as one of the two biographical notices puts it, and he retired to live the life of a recluse attached to the Monastery of Rabban Shabur, situated somewhere in south-west Iran. He is said to have become blind in old age.

Isaac was thus a younger contemporary of St Maximus the Confessor, and an older contemporary of St Bede. He was never formally canonized or included in any liturgical calendar until modern times; today, however, he is often referred to as 'Saint' Isaac and he now features in several church calendars. Fittingly,

---

[1] The *Book of Chastity* by the ninth-century East Syriac author Ishō'denah, published in Ishō'denah, *Le Livre de la Chasteté*, trans. and ed. by Jean-Baptiste Chabot, Mélanges d'archéologie et d'histoire 16 (École française de Rome, 1896), 53–4, para, 124; and an anonymous West Syriac source, the time and place of the writing of which are not known, published in *Studia Syriaca*, vol. 1, ed. by Ignatius Ephraem II Rahmani (Seminario Scharfensi, 1904), 32–3.

in view of his birthplace, the Greek Orthodox church in Qatar is dedicated to him, and an iconographic tradition has grown up.

Isaac's writings

Isaac's writings come down to us in the form of Collections of his Discourses, no doubt put together after his death; manuscripts containing them belong to all three Christian traditions: the Church of the East, the Syrian Orthodox, and the Chalcedonian Churches, Catholic and Orthodox. Since Isaac is said to have become blind in old age, it is possible that at least some of the Discourses may have been taken down in writing from his oral delivery. The number of Collections attributed to Isaac varies according to different sources; only three, however, would seem likely to be genuinely by Isaac. Of these three Collections, the First (with eighty-two Discourses) has long been known thanks to a Greek translation (of sixty-eight Discourses), made *c.* AD 800 at the Monastery of St Sabas near Jerusalem. This First Collection has proved to be influential, above all in subsequent Greek and Russian monastic tradition.

The existence of a Second Collection was already known to the Lazarist Father Paul Bedjan, who was the editor of the Syriac text of the First Collection (1909), but it was thought that the manuscript containing it had been destroyed during the massacres suffered by the Armenians and Syriacs during the First World War. In 1983, however, it was rediscovered—in the Bodleian Library, Oxford, where it had rested uncatalogued ever since it had been purchased in 1898 from the Reverend Yaroo Neesan, a member of the Archbishop of Canterbury's Educational Mission to the Church of the East in Urmi (north-west Iran). Before his visit to England Neesan had wisely had a copy of the manuscript made in 1895, to ensure that the contents remained available in Iran, where it eventually ended up in the library of the Chaldean bishop of Tehran, Mar Iohannan Issaye.

The Second Collection contains forty-one Discourses of which the third chapter consists of four sets of 'Centuries' entitled 'Headings (*Kephalaia*) on spiritual knowledge'; these take up about half of the entire text. A remarkable feature of the Second Collection lies in the final chapters where Isaac ponders on 'the mystery of Gehenna'.

Although the Second Collection was never translated into Greek, it was clearly known to Syriac-speaking Rum Orthodox[2] monks who included excerpts in monastic anthologies, such as *Sinai Syriac 14*.[3] At least parts of the Second Collection were translated into Arabic, and only recently some passages have been identified in Sogdian fragments discovered in the early twentieth century in Turfan (western China).

On a visit to Tehran the Jesuit scholar Michel van Esbroeck was able to photograph not only the manuscript dated 1895 of the Second Collection, but also a second manuscript dating from much the same time. On examination this turned out to contain a further sixteen Discourses by Isaac, constituting what is now known as the Third Collection.

Both the Second and the Third Collections contain some overlaps with Discourses in the First Collection: thus Discourses 16 and 17 of the Second Collection are the same as Discourses 54 and 55 in the First Collection; and in the Third Collection Discourses 14 and 15 are the same as Discourses 22 and 40 of the First Collection, while Discourse 17 is the same as Discourse 25 in the Second Collection.[4] Remarkably, chapter 10 of the Third Collection is in verse, and happens to be transmitted independently under the name of Ephrem; it is unlikely that either attribution is correct; in view of this, even though it consists

---

[2] That is, belonging to the Chalcedonian Orthodox Patriarchate of Antioch.
[3] Mount Sinai, St Catherine's Monastery, MS Sinai Syr. 14, containing an anthology of monastic texts.
[4] A basic guide to the three collections is provided in the Bibliography.

largely of a meditative prayer addressed to Christ, it is not included in the present collection of Isaac's prayers.

Although Isaac's discourses were intended for a monastic audience, and in several cases were specifically written for recluses, they nevertheless contain a great deal of insightful teaching which can be equally appreciated by the modern lay reader, seeing that Isaac has the remarkable gift of speaking over the centuries in a way that still remains very much alive and relevant.

Isaac's prayers

In the course of his writings Isaac provides three sets of sample prayers, two in the Second Collection (Chapters I and V) and the third in the Third Collection (chapter VII). Elsewhere, too, every now and then he bursts into prayer, and these additional prayers have here been collected together separately from three sets.

For the most part the prayers are addressed God or the Lord. In the former case it is sometimes clear that the Father is meant, but in others it is left ambiguous. Quite a number are addressed specifically to Christ, sometimes employing a traditional title such as 'Physician'. The final prayer of the second set concludes with reference to the Trinity. The Holy Spirit is only rarely specifically mentioned.

A considerable number of the rather longer prayers consist in reflections on particular aspects of salvation history, while many of the brief ones serve as 'arrow prayers'. The prayers take on various forms; especially common are requests: 'make...', or 'hold me worthy to...'. Of especial interest is one prayer (no. 104, below) commencing with the words 'may it be Your will...', wording that is often found in Jewish prayers. The participation of the body in prayer was important for Isaac, and so it is no surprise that some prayers are intended to be said while prostrated before the Cross. In a few cases Isaac specifies the occasion on which a particular prayer might be employed.

THE PRAYERS OF OF SAINT ISAAC OF NINEVEH

THREE SETS OF PRAYERS

(a) Second Collection, chapter 1 (II.1.80–93)[1]

When you pray attach the following to your prayer:

1. (II.1.80) O God, make me worthy to become aware of the hope that is reserved for the righteous at Your coming, when You will come [again] in our body to make known Your glory to the [two] worlds.

2. (II.1.81) O God, who brought Your love to the world even though it did not recognize You, and You were revealed to the righteous in part throughout all generations by means of the adumbrations of revelations, bring back to life the deadness of my stirrings, so that they become aware of You, in order that I may make haste to come to You and not pause until the hour when death sets the limit to my [life's] course in the haven of silence.

3. (II.1.82) O Christ, haven of mercies, who effected the revelation of Yourself in the midst of a sinful generation; for Whom the righteous awaited in their several generations, and Who was revealed in Your own time to the joy of the entire creation: grant to me different eyes, a different sense of hearing, and a different heart, so that, instead of the world, I may see,

---

[1] References are to the Collection number, followed by chapter and section numbers.

hear and perceive those things which are kept back by You for [*lit.* in] the revelation of Your glory to the race of Christians, by means of that sight, hearing and perception which is outside the ordinary [senses].

4. (II.1.83) Stir up in me, Lord, the taste of perception of You, so that I may be held worthy of [passing] from this world to You, seeing that the world has captivated me by its joys, [taking me] away from You. As long as my eyes rejoice at the sight of corruptible things, and my mind has a corporeal understanding, it is not possible for me to be completely free from the feeble feelings, subject to corruption, that [arise] out of them.

5. (II.1.84) Make me worthy, Lord, to encounter that [mode of] vision over which corruption holds no sway, so that, on encountering it, and becoming oblivious of the world and of myself, [all] corporeal images may be wiped out before my eyes.

6. (II.1.85) O Christ, the delight of our [human] race, the consolation of our impoverished condition, the support of our [human] nature's low estate, seeing how it has tottered and fallen, the hope of those deprived, the honourable Name that became known among humanity: accord a rising up for my fallen condition, effect a resurrection to my deadness, cause an awareness of life to stir within me, bring my soul out of the prison of ignorance, so that I may give thanks to Your name.[2] Blow upon my limbs with some of the air of the New Life; visit my corrupt state in the grave, and bring me out of

---

[2] Cf. Psalm 142:7. 'Blow upon' in the next sentence has in mind Ezekiel 37:5–6, and 9.

the place of darkness. May the dawn of the revelation of You visit me in the Sheol of ignorance. Human nature, endowed with speech, has grown silent in me: stir it once again, O Lord, to its natural vitality, for 'Sheol will not acknowledge You, nor will those who go down to the pit give praise to Your name'.[3] I have no tongue to utter that last thing, but may the living, such as me today, give thanks to You.[4]

The senses have grown dumb, the [heart's] stirrings have been silenced, thoughts have dried up, the entire operation of human nature in me is destitute of true life.

7. (II.1.86) There is no remembrance of You in me, there is no thanksgiving to You in the Sheol where I dwell, there is no joyful sound of the praises of You in my soul's lost state, all my limbs which are dead are awaiting the [birth] pangs of resurrection. There is no one who comes in to me in the desolation of Sheol.

8. (II.1.87) O my God, cause me to hear Your voice that resurrects all in a hidden way, decree for me in symbol the example of Lazarus, Your friend.[5] I know, Lord, that I have never been seen to be a diligent friend of Yours, [yet] I belong to Your flock, and my enemy has taken me off and humiliated me on earth. O God, make me worthy of a share in that magnificent state which You have prepared for Your friends in the Next World, and [likewise] of an awareness of the knowledge of Your love, and the inseparable union, and the indissoluble bond of the delight [that comes] from gazing upon You.

---

[3] Psalm 6:5.
[4] Cf. Psalm 115:16, but for 'the living', see LXX (113:26).
[5] Cf. John 11:11.

9. (II.1.88) O Lord, do not withhold from me Your acts of grace; may I not be deprived of the knowledge of You that is filled with hope.

10. (II.1.89) O Lord, save me from darkness of soul.

11. (II.1.90) O compassionate Christ, give me joy in Your hope: sow the hope of Yourself in my thoughts, and make me worthy of Your compassion when the revelation of You shines out from heaven. O Lord, may I not be required for the judgement of my wrongdoings when You come in Your glory.

12. (II.1.91) In Your grace, Lord, You brought me into being, and in Your grace You will hold my body worthy of resurrection; may my rising from the dust not be for judgement and shamefacedness.

13. (II.1.92) May I not be awakened [from the sleep of death] to endure judgement and deprivation of You; rather, awaken me from the dust to delight, O Lord, and to that glorious state to which Your will was intending to bring created rational beings from the very beginning, when You fashioned them.

You did not create me, Lord, for Gehenna's use: may I not become a vessel destined for perdition: perdition is for someone to be deprived of the utterly joy-giving vision of You, O Lord.

14. (II.1.93) Hold me worthy, Lord, of discovering the explanation of that hope for which You fashioned me in Your will from the very beginning, so that I may behold Your eternal glory; for it is You who, even before we came into being, wished in Your love that creation should come into being so as to become aware of You.

(b) Second Collection, chapter 5 (II.5.1–33)

[Preface]

The converse of hidden prayer, by St Isaac, which he drew up, arranged and composed with words of feeling and supplication, making, out of limbs joined together, a single body which will be useful for the meditation of hidden prayer: a person can be occupied with these words while standing up or sitting down, while working or while walking inside their cell, while going to sleep, until the point when sleep takes over, while they are in-doors, or while travelling on a journey, secretly occupying themselves with these words within their heart; likewise, while constantly kneeling on the ground, or wherever they happen to be standing, even if it is not in front of the Cross, and they will mingle the humility of their body with the stirrings of their prayer, for by these they will find benefit, as well as from those which they have laid down as their rule and from the place set aside, with the beneficial advantages which occur from it for them in the face of their changing state of mind and the times of peace and of vexations which come upon them. Thus, by making use of these prayers which have been appropriately composed so that they may find comfort, their soul will receive sanctification by them, and will be filled with the grace of the Spirit.

[Prayers]

15. (II.5.1) As my soul bows down to the ground I offer to You with all my bones and with all my heart the worship that befits You. O glorious God who dwells in ineffable silence, You have built for my renewal a tabernacle of love on earth where it is Your good pleasure to rest, a temple made of flesh and fashioned with the most holy sanctuary oil;[6] then You filled

---

[6] The reference is to the baptismal anointing.

it with Your holy presence so that all worship might be fulfilled in it, indicating the worship of the eternal persons of
Your Trinity and revealing to the worlds which You had
created in Your grace an ineffable mystery, a power which
cannot be felt or grasped by any part of Your creation that
has come into being. In wonder at it angelic beings are sub-
merged in silence, awed at the dark cloud[7] of this eternal
mystery and at the flood of glory which issues from within
this source of wonder, for it receives worship in the sphere
of silence from every intelligence that has been sanctified and
made worthy of You.

16. (II.5.2) I prostrate myself, Lord, at the footstool of Your feet[8]
and at Your holy right hand which has fashioned and made
me a human being capable of becoming aware of You. But I
have sinned and done wrong, both in myself and before You,
for I have abandoned holy converse with You and given over
my days to converse with the lusts. I beg of You, Lord, do not
set up against me the sins of my youth,[9] the ignorance of my
old age and the frailty of my nature which is too strong for
me and has caused me sink into reflection on things that are
hateful; rather, turn my heart towards You, away from the
troublesome distraction of the lusts; cause to dwell in me a
hidden light. Your acts of goodness towards me always an-
ticipate any kind of volition on my part to do well and any
readiness for virtue on the part of my heart. You have never
held back Your care in order to test my free will; rather, as
with the care of a father towards his young son, so has Your

---

[7] Cf. Exodus 20:21.
[8] Cf. Psalm 99:5; 132:7.
[9] Cf. Psalm 25:7.

care for me run after me; Your fatherly graciousness has visited my frailty and has had no intention of making test of my will, for You knew all the time that, even less than a child, I do not know whither I am travelling.

17. (II.5.3) I beseech You, O God, send me help from your highest heavens so that I may keep afar from my heart every evil intention and every carnal wish. Do not cast me, Lord, from Your protection lest my adversary find me and trample upon me just as he desires, destroying me utterly. It is You who grant repentance and a sorrowing heart to the sinner who repents; in this way You ease the heart of the weight of sin that is laid upon it, thanks to the comfort which comes from sorrowing and from the gift of tears.

18. (II.5.4) At the door of Your compassion do I knock, Lord; send aid to my scattered impulses which are intoxicated with the multitude of the passions and the power of darkness. You can see my sores hidden within me: stir up contrition—though not corresponding to the weight of my sins, for if I receive full awareness of the extent of my sins, Lord, my soul would be consumed by the bitter pain from them. Assist my feeble stirrings on the path to true repentance, and may I find alleviation from the vehemence of sins through the contrition that comes of Your gift, for without the power of Your grace I am quite unable to enter within myself, become aware of my stains, and so, at the sight of them, be able to be still from great distraction.

19. (II.5.5) O name of Jesus, key to all gifts, open up for me the great door to Your treasure-house so that I may enter and praise You with the praise that comes from the heart in return for Your mercies which I have experienced in latter days; for You came and renewed me with an awareness of the Next World.[10]

20. (II.5.6) I give praise to Your holy nature, Lord, for You have made my nature a sanctuary for Your hiddenness and a tabernacle for Your mysteries, a place where You can dwell, and a holy temple for Your divinity, namely for Him who holds the sceptre of Your kingdom, who governs all that You have brought into being, the glorious tabernacle of Your eternal being, the source of renewal for the ranks of fire which minister to You, the way to knowledge of You, the wisdom — Jesus Christ the Only-Begotten from Your bosom,[11] and the remnant[12] gathered in from Your creation, both visible and spiritual.

21. (II.5.7) O Mystery, exalted beyond every word and beyond silence, who became human in order to renew us by means of voluntary union with the flesh, reveal to me the path by which I may be raised up to Your mysteries, travelling along a course that is clear and tranquil, free from the illusions of this world. Gather my mind into the silence of prayer, so that wandering thoughts may be silenced within me during that luminous converse of supplication and mystery-filled wonder.

22. (II.5.8) I prostrate myself, Lord, at the throne of Your majesty, I who am dust and ashes[13] and the dregs of humanity. A thousand upon thousands of angels and countless legions

---

[10] Cf. Matthew 18:28 (Peshitta: 'New World').
[11] Cf. John 1:18.
[12] Cf. Isaiah 1:9, Romans 9:29.
[13] Cf. Genesis 18:17 (Abraham).

of Seraphim offer You, the holy nature hidden from the senses and knowledge of all created beings, spiritual worship in the hiddenness of their natures with their fiery praises and their holy impulses; for You are close at hand, Lord, with Your assistance to everyone at all times of need, and Your door is open in season and out of season[14] for the entreaties of all. You do not abhor sinners nor does Your majesty feel abhorrence for the souls which are stained with all kinds of sins; rather, You draw up everyone from endless evils, including me, Lord, who am utterly defiled, seeing that You have held me worthy to fall down before You on my face and make bold to pronounce Your holy name with my mouth, even though I am a vessel full of uncleanness and not worthy to be numbered among the children of Adam. Grant me, Lord, that I may be made holy by praising You, and be made pure by the remembrance of You; renew my life with a transformation of mind and with beneficial thoughts which You, in Your grace, stir within me. Be a guide to my mind in my meditations on You, and make me forget my stumbling conduct through a renewal of mind which You instil in me. Stir up within me requests that are beneficial, with my will in accordance with Your will, for it is You who give prayer to those who pray. Imprint in me a single will, one which gazes towards You at all times, and a deliberation which is never weakened in its hope of You by continual deaths for Your sake. Grant, Lord, that I do not pray before You with unfeeling words just uttered with the lips, but may I be spread prostrate on the ground in hidden humility of heart and repentance of mind.

---

[14] Cf. 2 Timothy 4:2.

23. (II.5.9) O God, who in Your forbearing at my sins grants me life in this world, do not deprive me of the life of the world to come which is awaited with hope by those who supplicate You here in wretchedness.

24. (II.5.10) O Christ, whose love has set the saints apart from family, kin, and humanity's life of ease, and in whom the strength of the natural passions has become silent in the face of the sweetness of this love, grant me, O Lord, to renounce my life out of desire for You, and may I be found to be dead during my lifetime to all things that give pleasure in this world; and through Your might, O Lord, may the storms which are kindled in my limbs be silenced, and may Your love separate me from the world and from converse with it. Portray in my mind an image which cannot be seen, by which the impulse of all the sweetness of recollections of the temporal world and its images may be overcome.

25. (II.5.11) I kneel before Your majesty and prostrate myself on the ground before You, O God, for without my having asked You or even having existed, You brought me into existence; before You fashioned me in the womb[15] You knew that I would live a life full of tumult and backsliding, yet You did not refrain from creating me and granting me all the attributes with which You have honoured human nature, even though You knew beforehand my evils. You are aware of my requests even before they become known to me, and of my prayers even before they have been prayed before You: grant to me, O my God, at this hour whatever You are aware that my wretched nature needs in its present

---

[15] Cf. Isaiah 44:2, 49:5.

peril. You are aware of my soul's affliction, and in Your
hands lies its healing.

26. (II.5.12) O Power, whereby the Fathers of old overcame the
mighty and fearsome attacks of the rebellious one—people
who, though sharing in human nature which is subject to
many needs, were like those without need, manifesting on
earth a likeness of things to come, while You made human
tombs, caves and crevices the tabernacle of Your revelations
to them: pour into my heart the fervour of their thoughts, so
that by it I may become valiant and trample on natural desire
and on the fear of all that opposes human nature; sow in me
a knowledge of humility and an unrestrainable impetus for
the acute journey towards You. O Refuge of the weak, straight
path for those who are held back by wandering astray, place
of escape for all who are caught in storms, lay low the adversary's boast over me, subdue the strength of his cunning
actions against me, bring low his exalted pride, make
smooth[16] Your hidden paths before my thoughts, and be for
me a comfort in the time of my anguish and a guide in the
place of peril.

27. (II.5.13) O Sun of righteousness,[17] by which the righteous
have beheld their own selves and become a mirror for their
generations, open up within me the gate to awareness of You;
grant me a joyful mind, one which sails above the rocks of
error, until I may reach that serene abode, as did our Fathers
of old who pleased You with their discerning lives.

---

[16] Cf. Isaiah 45:13.
[17] Cf. Malachi 3:20.

28. (II.5.14) Sanctify me by Your mysteries, illumine my mind with knowledge of You, make Your hope to shine out in my heart, hold me worthy to supplicate for it, O God my Father and Lord of my life; illumine Your lamp within me, place in me what belongs to You so that I may forget what belongs to myself. Cast upon me the constraint of wonder at You, so that the constraint of nature may be overpowered by it. Stir up within me the vision of Your mysteries so that I may become aware of what was placed in me at holy baptism. You have placed within me a guide: may he show me Your glory at all times. You made me to be light and salt for the world:[18] may I not prove a stumbling-block for my companions. Seeing that I have left the world, may I never again look back to it and to the things which I renounced when I made my promise to You. Cast reins of delight upon my heart, so that my senses may not gaze beyond the paths of Your law. Rig together my impulses for the ship of repentance, so that in it I may exult as I travel over the world's sea until I reach the haven of Your hope. When I am tempted, may my mind take courage from the recollection of You. Illumine before me the path that is dark by means of the brilliance of awareness of You.

29. (II.5.15) O God, hold me worthy of insight into the mystery of Your love which is depicted in Your dispensation for the perceptible world in the works of Your creation, and in the mystery of the killing of Your beloved Son.

30. (II.5.16) Our Creator, who are aware of the sick state of my nature,[19] hold back from me the violence of the adversary;

---

[18] Cf. Matthew 5:13–14.
[19] Cf. Romans 5:6, Hebrews 4:15.

beat off from my limbs the upsurge of sin; cause its heat to abate from my heart, proffer the hand of healing to my soul's prostrate state; bind up my inner senses with the bandage of the Cross; increase in me abundance of the love for You that comes from insight into the Crucified One; draw my mind inwards with the hidden things of the mysteries which the Cross bears; fix within me a remembrance of the humility of Your beloved Son; increase within me wonder at Your dispensation for me.

31. (II.5.17) O God, who, even before You had brought reconciliation to the world You gave to it Your Only-Begotten, and after You had brought reconciliation You caused it to inherit the throne of Your divinity, do not abandon me to go to the grave without hope, and may I not sit with the fetters of my sins in darkness like one who is dead for ever.[20]

32. (II.5.18) We give thanks to You, O God, for Your gift to the world, a gift whose richness created beings are not capable of describing; seeing that I too am part of that world, may I not begrudge my portion of thanksgiving which I owe to You. For this reason I will praise You and confess Your name. You have given Your entire treasure to the world: if You gave the Only-Begotten from Your bosom[21] and from the throne of Your being for the benefit of all, what further do You have which You have not given to Your creation? The world has become mingled with God, and creation and Creator have become one! Praise to You for Your inscrutable purpose: truly this mystery is vast! Glory to You for Your mysteries which

---

[20] Cf. Psalm 143:3.
[21] John 1:18.

are hidden from us. Make me worthy, Lord, to taste of this great mystery which is hidden and concealed, a mystery of which the world is not yet worthy to perceive. Maybe You indicated something of it to Your saints who live in the body above the world and who are at all times above the impulses of the flesh.

33. (II.5.19) The flood of Christ's mysteries presses upon my mind like the waves of the sea: I wanted to be silent before them, and not speak, but they proved to be like burning fire that was kindled in my bones. My mind rebukes me, revealing to me my sins. Your mystery stupefies me, but urges me on to behold it: in silence it indicates to me, 'Do not be slow to approach because you are afraid of your sins, O sinner, for it is by meditating upon this that the mud of sin will be shaken off your mind'.

34. (II.5.20) O Unbinder of our nature, unbind from me the hidden bonds which have been cast around my interior limbs, and undo from kind from me the hidden bonds which have been cast around my interior limbs, and undo from my outer senses the manifest restraints, so that I may hasten to enter the Paradise if Your mysteries and to eat of the Tree of Life from which Adam was not allowed to eat.[22]

35. (II.5.21) O my Saviour, preserve me from the delusion of the demons; O my God, keep far from me laxity of purpose; O my Hope, pour into my heart the inebriation which consists in the hope of You. O Jesus Christ, the resurrection and light of all worlds, place the crown of knowledge of You upon

---

[22] Genesis 3:22.

my soul's head; open up suddenly before me the door of
mercies; cause the rays of Your grace to shine out in my heart;
be a guide to the feet of my thoughts, until I reach Sion, Your
holy mountain. Make me worthy of that holy city which the
saints have entered at the end of their journey.

My Creator and my hope, the anchor[23] of my life in the
midst of storms, the staff for my feeble condition, the honour
of my dishonourable state, who raises my head which is bent
down to the ground, do not deliver me over to the desire of
my adversary; do not provide an opportunity for his shame-
lessness. Place a great chasm[24] in front of him to prevent him
crossing over to me and perturbing me. Hold me worthy to
complete my short and fleeting life in the service of You; may
I be found close to You at the end of my days, may I be found
in Your vineyard at the sunset of my life.

Make me worthy, before the time of crossing over, of the
embossed coin which You vouchsafed to the labourers.[25] Out
of grace, Lord, and not because of my service, hold me worthy even at the eleventh hour of my life to be found diligently
in Your service. May the world not captivate me with its
harmful occupations, and may it not confine me in the cage
of its cares.

36. (II.5.22) O Christ, who are covered with light as though with
a garment,[26] who for my sake stood naked in front of Pilate,
clothe me with that might which You caused to overshadow
the saints, whereby they conquered this world of struggle.

---

[23] Cf. Hebrews 6:19.
[24] Cf. Luke 16:26.
[25] Cf. Matthew 20:9–10.
[26] Cf. Psalm 104:3.

May Your divinity, Lord, take pleasure in me, and lead me above the world to be with You.

37. (II.5.23) O Christ, upon whom the many-eyed Cherubim are unable to look because of the glory of Your countenance, yet out of Your love You received spit upon Your face: remove the shame from my face and grant an open face before You at the time of prayer.

38. (II.5.24) O Christ, because of our nature's sin You went out into the wilderness[27] and vanquished the ruler of darkness, taking from him the victory after five thousand years;[28] force to flee from me him who at all times forces the human race to sin.

39. (II.5.25) May the Cross of shame which You mounted for my sake become a bridge to that peaceful abode; may the crown of thorns[29] with which Your head was crowned become for me the helmet of salvation[30] on the heated day of battle; may the spit which Your face received[31] prepare me to have an open face before the tribunal at Your advent; may Your holy body which was exposed on the Cross crucify me to this world and its lusts by means of love for You; may Your clothing for which lots were cast[32] tear asunder before my eyes the garment of darkness with which I am inwardly clothed; may the water and blood which came

---

[27] Cf. Matthew 4:1.

[28] Isaac follows the tradition, familiar to the Greek and Syriac Fathers, that the Incarnation took place at the end of the fifth millennium.

[29] Matthew 27:29.

[30] Ephesians 6:17.

[31] Matthew 26:67, 27:30.

[32] Matthew 27:35.

forth from Your side[33] become for me a document granting liberty[34] from the ancient state of servitude; may Your Body and Your Blood which have been mingled with my body remain within me as a pledge that I will not be deprived of the constant sight of You in that realm which has no end; may the mysteries of the faith which I have preserved uncorrupted in myself preserve for me something to glory about on that day when the world is made ready to receive Your advent, and may they replace there the inadequacy of my ascetic conduct.

40. (II.5.26) May there be remembered, Lord, on Your holy altar at the fearful moment when Your body and Your blood are sacrificed for the salvation of the world, all the fathers and brethren who are on mountains, in caves,[35] in ravines, cliffs, rugged and desolate places, who are hidden from the world, and it is only known to You where they are — those who have died and those still living and ministering before You in body and soul, You the Holy One who dwell in the holy ones[36] in whom Your divinity finds rest; those who have abandoned the temporal world and have already become dead to its life in that they have gone out in search of You, seeking You with yearning amidst the afflictions of their weary state.

O Sovereign of all worlds and of all the orthodox Fathers who, for the sake of the truth of the faith, have endured exile and afflictions at the hands of persecutors, who in monasteries, convents, deserts and the habitations of the world,

---

[33] John 19:34.
[34] Cf. Romans 8:21.
[35] Cf. Hebrews 11:38.
[36] Cf. Isaiah LXX (57:15).

everywhere and in every place, have made it their care to please You with labours for the sake of virtue: accompany them with Your assistance, Lord, and be a helmet for them always, send them continual comfort in secret, and bind their minds close to You in all their struggles; may the power of Your Trinity dwell in them, and may they minister to You right up to the end of their lives with a good conscience and with a good manner of life. Hold them worthy while they are still in the body of the harbour of rest. And to those who are encountering hard battles with the demons, whether openly or in secret, send succour, Lord, and overshadow them with the cloud[37] of Your grace; place on their mind's head the helmet of salvation,[38] bring low the power of the enemy before them, and may the might of Your right hand support them at all times lest they grow weak in their thoughts, failing to gaze continually towards You; clothe them in the armour of humility, that a sweet fragrance may waft from them at all times, giving pleasure to Your will.

41. (II.5.27) May those who suffer from dire sicknesses and grievous illnesses of the body also be remembered before You; send to them an angel of compassion and assuage their souls which are so tormented by their bodies' terrible afflictions. Have pity, too, Lord, on those who are subjected to the hands of evil, wicked and godless men; send to them speedily an angel of compassion and save them from their plight. O my Lord and my God, send comfort to all those who are constrained by whatever kind of hardship.

---

[37] Cf. Exodus 13:21.
[38] Ephesians 6:17.

42. (II.5.28) O Lord, overshadow Your holy Church which has been redeemed by Your blood; cause to dwell in her Your true peace which You gave to Your holy apostles;[39] bind her children in holy bonds of indissoluble love; may the rebel not have power over her, and keep far from her persecution, tumult, and wars, both from those within and from those without; and may kings and priests be bound together in great peace and love, their minds always filled with gazing towards You; and may the holy faith be a wall for Your flock. And hold me too, a sinner, worthy through their prayers of being preserved always under the mighty protection of Your holy arm which is Your providential care that encompasses all, Amen.

43. (II.5.29) I beg and beseech You, Lord, grant to all who have gone astray a true knowledge of You, so that each and every one may come to know Your glory.

44. (II.5.30) In the case of all who have passed from this world lacking a virtuous life and having had no faith, be an advocate for them, Lord, for the sake of the body which You took from them, so that from the single united body of the world we may offer up praise to Father, Son and Holy Spirit in the Kingdom of heaven, an unending source of eternal delight.

[Epilogue: II.5.31–3]

Those who wait expectantly to receive in their inner person the grace of the Holy Spirit should engage continually in meditations and supplicatory converse such as these: by such converse they will become sanctified, and with an intent such as this they will be held worthy of a gift from on high.

---

[39] Cf. John 14:27.

We should pray with suffering, and we should make supplication to God for all these things with pain. And this is the attitude we should have towards all human beings: we should pray for them with suffering, as for ourselves, for in this way the Divinity will come and rest in us and cause His will to reside in us 'as in heaven, so on earth'.[40]

You too, our brother, should have this aim in prayer and meditation all your days, both when you are kneeling on the ground, and during the rest of the other hours of the day in a hidden way within your heart. Even though you may not want to use the same sequence and order of words, the aim in prayer should certainly be the same all the time, namely that we may be held worthy, by means of this intent and meditation, of the gift which was received by our fathers whose bodies and souls had become temples for the Holy Spirit.

(c) Third Collection, chapter 7 (III.7.1–48)

45. (III.7.1) I bow down to Your majesty, O God, for You have created me in Your love, and in Christ You have delivered me from spiritual darkness, which is the soul's ignorance of You. You have caused the time of error to pass from us, so that we no longer walk, as if in the night, in our knowledge concerning You, as was the case in those former generations of old.

46. (III.7.2) Praise to You who bore our wicked deeds in Your mercy, who puts to right our sinful state in Your compassion, who removes our defects in Your kindness. You have granted

---

[40] Matthew 6:10.

to us the possibility of believing in You in a way that befits Your majesty, and You have not paid attention to our ingratitude before You on every occasion, for You are the compassionate God, and You continually overcome the flaring up of our sins with the dew of Your grace.

47. (III.7.3) What mouth is adequate to sing Your praises, what tongue is sufficient to laud You, for You have restrained our sins through the abundance of Your grace, and instead of sentencing sinners, You have dispensed from Your treasury. For it is not to enter into judgement with us[41] that You desire, but to bring us closer to You, for we are Your creation. Your grace surpasses the measure of our knowledge, and so the wondrous nature of the angels will give You praise instead of us, for it is in them that You have placed the strength that is capable of receiving the wondrous stirring of Your Sanctity.

48. (III.7.4) Let the angels give thanks to You on our behalf, for our human nature is too feeble for due thanksgiving to You. May they mingle into the wondrous stirrings of their own songs of praise also thanksgiving on our behalf. They grieved at our becoming lost from You,[42] when You cut us off from mingling with them in the matter of knowledge concerning Your hidden being. But You have given us, without our asking, the great gift of faith, by which we may draw near to the mysteries of Divine Knowledge—mysteries by which the spiritual beings progressively take steps up towards the presence of Your Being.

---

41 Cf. Psalm 143:2.
42 Contrast Luke 15:10.

49. (III.7.5) It is by means of the mysteries of faith that those to whom You are close by in faith, though not in vision,[43] are conveyed within mind and comes with great knowledge; for this faith is something which You grant as a gift to rational beings so that their thoughts may ponder on the mysteries that You reveal to them in Your love, so that they may have faith in that which is unattainable and unknowable, namely the Divine Nature which is hidden from all.

50. (III.7.6) Conviction concerning this, O eternal God, cannot be found anywhere within creation, either by the spiritual be-ings, or by the feeble human race, except only if it comes from the fountain of Your love which You open up continuously for the hosts above and for those below, seeing that, in accor-dance with the measure of each of these ranks, You open up the treasury of Your mercies in revelations for them that in-volve a greater or lesser spiritual knowledge.

51. (III.7.7) The gift of Your grace is required as an intermediary which will raise up our intellect into the converse of faith in You. Because of the great cloud of obscurity surrounding Your Sanctity, even the eyes of the Cherubim are too dis-turbed in their vision to gaze within the hidden place of the cloud of the Divine Glory.[44]

52. (III.7.8) Unless to a greater or smaller extent they are as-sisted by Your grace to ascend to the summit of faith, spiritual knowledge consists in the rays which diffuse over the intellect, coming from the awesome fire which flashes out from the interior place of faith. This place is called the

---

[43] 2 Corinthians 5:7.
[44] Cf. Exodus 20:21.

Interior Sanctuary of the revered honour of the glorious nature of the Divine Being—a sanctuary into which not a single created being has ever entered, or will enter, apart from the One who was sanctified so as to enter in the foreknowledge of God,[45] in accordance with His good purpose to make propitiation at every moment on behalf of all the sins of His people.

53. (III.7.9) For it is by faith that a person enters into a place that is more interior than that of the watchers.[46] Through one of them on a single occasion mercy caused Him to enter and be seated there.[47] From that point onwards He gives authority to human intellects that have been made holy to enter into it—I mean, by faith and the power that comes from it; for it is unattainable and withdrawn from even a momentary glimpse. As with us, this applies also to the eyes of angels. In revelation, they are ahead of us and much closer—until You are revealed for our liberation.

54. (III.7.10) O True hope of ours, the delight of our human race, the pride of our human nature, the sure advocate of our weak state; more potent than Israel's sacrifices is Your intercession on our behalf. If the flesh of animals, and the ashes when they have been burnt, used without any doubt to purify and sanctify those on whose behalf they were being sacrificed, how much more do You purify us at all times, being an interior offering offered up on behalf of the world.[48]

----

45 Hebrews 9:11–12.
46 That is, angels; cf. Daniel 4:13.
47 Cf. Hebrews 9:11–12.
48 Cf. Romans 12:1; Hebrews 9:13–14.

55. (III.7.11) You are the One who offers up, and You are the One who makes propitiation; You are the priest, and You are the One who is consecrated; You are the Sacrifice, and You are the One who receives it. If the speechless metal leaf—which manifested the symbol of Your humanity—used to grant forgiveness to supplications,[49] how much more so are You, the glorious image of the Godhead; if Your symbols were pouring forth upon the needy such wealth, how much more will You, the true prototype of symbols, pour forth Your mercies upon us!

56. (III.7.12) For it is for You that the prophets and kings in their several times have been awaiting, along with the righteous in their generations. It is not just Your day, O Expectation of the gentiles, but we have received You in our very hands, and we rejoice in You. They were the ones who beheld You in their revelations, and in their wonder they yearned for You, whereas we behold the interpretation of their symbols. You have poured out upon us the Gihon[50] of Your grace, O our Creator! You have opened up Your entire treasury in our time, and we have access to it. You have manifested to us the symbols of Your Christ. It was by a desire for His coming that the many generations of old were gripped, but they passed on without receiving comfort, in that His days were far distant from their times.

57. (II.7.13) Turn back, my soul, to your source of rest,[51] for you have beheld the hope of all peoples, you have carried Him upon your very hands, you have been absolved by Him of

---

[49] Cf. Exodus 25:17, 21–2; Leviticus 16:13–15. For the significance of the metal leaf, see Second Collection XI.14.

[50] One of the four rivers of Paradise, Genesis 2:17.

[51] Psalm 116:7.

your iniquity and of all your sins. Bless the Lord, O my soul, along with all my bones, bless His holy name.[52] O my soul, praise the Lord;[53] may I praise the Lord while I live and sing to my God as long as I have my being.[54] O my heart and my flesh, praise the living God![55]

58. (III.7.14) I will praise You, Lord, and my tongue shall proclaim Your righteousness as I give praise the whole day,[56] since You have brought me closer to the Majesty of Your lordship, and You have allowed me to share in the praises of the angels, mingling me with the celebrations of their assemblies. You have not deprived me, Lord, of this sharing with them, which consists in faith, for such is the nature of all the spiritual beings—of the wings of the watchers and the mirror of their revelations. Our sharing with the angels and our mingling with their assemblies consists in our conforming our will with theirs, in the spirit of the faith we have received.

59. (III.7.15) This is the glory of the spiritual beings, and the power of the wondrous revelations concerning the Godhead, along with the changing experiences of faith that spring up in their stirrings, since You are experienced by them by faith and not by sight.[57] Your hidden and holy Nature is not subject to touch or sight by a single created being: it is by faith that created natures take delight in the rays that flash out in their natural state as a result of Your mercy.

---

[52] Psalm 103:1.
[53] Psalm 146:1–2.
[54] Psalm 104:33.
[55] Psalm 84:3.
[56] Psalm 71:5.
[57] Cf. 2 Corinthians 5:7.

60. (III.7.16) It is to the mysteries of this glory that You have brought us close through Your Beloved Son, for You have let us approach the foothills of the mountain of faith—the mountain in whose midst there dwell the nine ranks of the hosts of spiritual beings, and at its summit is built Your holy city.

61. (III.7.17) O our God, living and life-giving, Your apostle and servant Paul proclaimed to us about this mountain when he said 'You have been brought close'.[58] You have been brought close to the mountain of Sion—which is faith and knowledge of the Lord—and to the city of the living God, to the Jerusalem which is in heaven. This is something which consists in participation in Divine Contemplation with the myriad assemblies of angels. For the mind which shares in the revelation with them is on the ascent of the ladder of faith up to Sion, the mountain of God.

62. (III.7.18) With the sum of our misfortunes You have brought us to this, O God, the Just Judge[59] who are not always angered, but who turn away Your gaze from our sins.[60] You did not spare Your Beloved Son, but on behalf of us all[61] You handed Him over so that His death might be the source of our justification. In Your Christ You have made known to us the hidden matters of Your eternal wisdom,[62] and brought us to the knowledge of faith in You.[63]

---

[58] Hebrews 12:22.
[59] Psalm 9:5.
[60] Psalm 85:5–7.
[61] Romans 8:22.
[62] Psalm 51:8.
[63] Romans 16:25–6.

63. (III.7.19) Do not abandon me, leaving me stripped of those mercies which have come upon me, for You invited me and brought me close to the realm of Your glory[64]—without my begging You—out of Your eternal love. Let me not be deprived of a loving meditation on this glory. O Lord, send to my aid Your strength to assist me and draw me up out of the sea of temporal existence. O Ocean of help, stay and assist me, do not abandon me in the depths of ills.

64. (III.7.20) O Guide of life, show to my mind the path towards You: open the door of mindfulness of You before my thoughts. O renewer of all, renew me with the knowledge of You, stir up in my heart a genuine hope in You. O Ocean of compassion, draw me up from the troubled state caused by distraction away from You. Cause me to enter into the burning fire of faith in You, cause me to drink of the wine of the apperception of hope in You. Hold me worthy of that fervour of heart that burns unceasingly once the drop of hope in You has fallen upon it.

65. (III.7.21) Who has ever received the thought of this and is able to endure in the face of its might? Who has ever tasted it and remembered themselves any more? What body, or what thought, can endure the fragrance of faith in You? O Christ, the goal of truth, cause Your truth to shine out in our hearts.[65] O Might who shone out in the saints, in the love of You may I overcome the world[66] and its delights. O Might who put on our body, cause insights into Your truth to shine out in my

---

[64] 1 Thessalonians 2:12.
[65] 2 Corinthians 4:6.
[66] 1 John 4:4; 5:4.

darkened soul. O Ocean that supports the world, draw me up from the stormy sea!

66. (III.7.22) You know, Lord, that I grieve at my sins each day in Your presence: hidden tears spring up in me as I look upon my soul's feeble nature. And when I want to heal my sins through groans, bad desires rush in with them, so as to change my pain of heart, bringing about my downfall, ruining my course of thought, dragging it away from supplication and concentration on You.

67. (III.7.23) You are the physician who is well aware of the convulsions of my heart. Give strength to my heart in the face of the passions within it, for You know that it is not in my ability to overcome in this battle: it is Your might that will conquer and bring the victory in me: bring the victory in me, as is Your wont, and consider the victory to be mine in accordance with Your wisdom! For in the case of those who have vanquished, their victory has been along these lines.

68. (III.7.24) Let my heart's compunction be a witness in Your presence that the commotion caused by the flesh is stronger than my volition.

69. (III.7.25) While every day I weep over things past, there is no time when I do not bear the very same faults which simply renew those for which I offer repentance. O Victor, who gives victory to those who are defeated—seeing that their natural condition can never be victorious, grant me that strength which accords victory to human nature: while defeat comes from within itself, the Victorious One in His grace calls out to it, since it never knows the experience of victory coming from itself.

70. (III.7.26) Another power weaves a garment for human nature,[67] the same power which in wisdom fashioned its weak character for the purpose of revealing His goodness, being aware of how easily it would change, His aim being that it would be set in the right with the forgiveness of faults which He grants unrestrainedly, in order thereby to make manifest the goodness of His nature. Thus the weak character of human nature would be the means of proclaiming His kindness, and a witness to His mercies.[68]

71. (III.7.27) May meditation on awareness of You overcome the difficulties of the struggle.

May the sweet converse of hope in You captivate me instead of my consenting to the flesh.

May the delight of the knowledge of You separate me from the way of human nature. Hold me worthy, Lord, of insights into Truth which concern Your will with respect to us. Hold me worthy of that meditation during the course of which it alters the form of our thoughts, so that they can see into the next world that is unlike the present one.

72. (III.7.28) May the Power, which has taught me to seek after these matters, place in me a taste of the love for them; seeing that You have brought me close to You through sowing them in my senses, accomplish in me, within my spirit, the experiencing of what this means.

73. (III.7.29) Seeing that You have allowed me to share, in a mystery, in the glory of Your divinity, strengthen within me the hope for it by means of the assurance of faith. Because

---

67 Cf. 2 Timothy 4:8.
68 2 Corinthians 12:9.

You have brought me, O Lord, close to this understanding by means of Your Beloved, teach me in a hidden way what I should think about Your majesty. Grant to me a healthy mind that blossoms all the time with a luminous reflection that is directed towards You.

74. (III.7.30) Remove from me that stupid mentality which thinks only in an infantile manner; stir up in me instead those things that are right to think about Your glorious nature, so that I do not begin to give praise concerning Your Divine Judgements after the manner of the human mentality which is subject to the passions, thinking along the lines of the human passions concerning Your saving purpose for our souls. Tread out in me the paths to Your wisdom, open up for me the door to meditation on Your glorious will, for I do not know, Lord, how to enter into it.

75. (III.7.31) O Christ, the door to mysteries, allow me to share in the apperception of Your mysteries; in You, Lord, may I enter to the Father, and may I receive in my stirrings the grace of Your Holy Spirit. O Christ, the key to the mysteries and the sum of all mysteries, in You may there be opened up for us the doorway to the mysteries that have from eternity been hidden in Your Father, for in Your dispensation is hidden the ocean of all mysteries.

76. (III.7.32) Hold me worthy to receive You within myself so that, in You, I may open the door and enter into these mysteries, both past and future. O Lord, make me worthy of the sweetness of hope in You: whoever tastes of this cup will then persevere in controlling themselves and will return to their true self; for like pressed grape-juice it becomes sweet in the heart of those who receive it.

77. (III.7.33) O Renewer of all, renew me with the apperception of hope in You, the joy of all creation. Hold me worthy of that joy which springs up beyond the world of the flesh and is received in the silence of the soul. Bury within my limbs the fire of Your love, cast the bonds of wonder at You on my heart, bind my mind's stirrings in the silence of the knowledge of You—for knowledge of You consists entirely in silence. Hold me worthy to gaze upon You with opened eyes, with eyes that are more interior than those of the body.

78. (III.7.34) Create new eyes within me, O You who created new eyes for the blind man;[69] block my external ears, but open up the hidden ears which listen to the silence and are attentive to the Spirit, so that from Your Spirit I may hear the word of silence which springs up in the heart, but is not written there, which is stirred up in the mind, but is not spoken—though spoken by the lips of the Spirit, which is heard with a hearing that is other than that of the body. O Ocean of pity, take me and wash from me the filth of my fallen nature, and make me a vessel that is of use in Your Sanctuary.

79. (III.7.35) O Lord, You did not make me like a potter's vessel which, once broken, cannot be mended, or, when it has become encrusted, cannot regain its former polish, as when it was new. Rather, You created me in Your wisdom like objects of gold or silver which, when tarnished, can—with the refining of the pain of compunction—once again imitate the colour of the sun and shine out. By means of the crucible of repentance it can be brought back to its former condition. In You, O Craftsman, who polishes and renews our human

---

[69] John 9.

nature, because I have sullied the beauty acquired at baptism and become defiled, in You may I receive a more excellent beauty. In You is the beauty of creation, for You have turned creation back once more to its beauty that was snatched away from it in paradise.

80. (III.7.36) O New sun, light up Your lamp in my darkened mind; O Christ who has caused creation's weeping to pass away, grant to me hidden tears and weeping that belong within the discerning eyes of the mind. Their moisture does not trickle down from the body, rather, it represents the heat of hidden repentance, which conveys a true joy within the mind, a consolation that silences the mouth and extends to the heart unwonted sustenance, establishing it as a true interior witness which testifies to it at all times concerning the pledge of the forgiveness of sins which, through mercy, it has received.[70]

81. (III.7.37) My sins are many, O Lord, but Your compassion is greater than the extent of my sins. My wicked actions are grievous, but they are not to be compared with Your mercy: however grievous my wrongdoings, Your love is greater than them. I gaze on my sins, O Lord, and I am dumbfounded at how audacious I have been. When I consider Your actions regarding me, astonishment takes hold of me, how I have been treated by You in the opposite way to what I deserve.

82. (III.7.38) Your gift has brought me to a knowledge of You, and not to chastisement from You. In Your mercy You have caused me to drink of Your sweetness—not because of any

---

[70] Cf. 2 Corinthians 1:21–2, 5:5; Ephesians 1:13–14.

ascetic labours on my part. You have clothed me in feeble human nature which is a daily witness to Your grace; Your wisdom, by means of our weakness, shows us Your love towards us. You placed in us a propensity to backsliding, in order that it should be a testimony concerning our human nature. Your patience towards us extends far beyond our wrongdoings and sins.

83. (III.7.39) It was not that You found patience as a device for the greater expectation of our torment: we should not think of the good which is in Your very nature as the cause of evil: ignorance may suggest this to us; if this stirring should dare to appear in us, You put up with it unperturbed. And it is not because You are constrained by any difficulties that You carry our sins.

84. (III.7.40) It is easy for You to bear our wickedness, just as it was easy for You to bring our creation into being from nothing. For us both things seem difficult—seeing that we are not capable of bearing even a small sin on the part of our neighbour when we see it. We even judge, O Lord, with our own kind of judgement the great ocean of Your love which surpasses, with its waves, the measure of all our evil-doing. In accordance with our human mentality we suppose that You too are under constraint when You, our maker, bear up with us. Our suffering acts as a mirror for us, and on the basis of what belongs to us we see things, and we weigh up, O Lord, Your opulence against the sufferings of human beings.

85. (III.7.41) Grant us, Lord, a knowledge to look on You as You are and not as we are; and may we think about You in a way that is appropriate for You, O Giver of all gifts. Your great generosity towards us consists in this: a knowledge of the reality which Your total hiddenness is stirring within us. For Your goodness, Lord, and Your love, and the power of good which is in Your nature, is the cause of Your taking up the burden of our sins; and in addition to this, even if You are not expecting a sinner's repentance, You nevertheless grant them the time to repent.

86. (III.7.42) In our understanding of the Scriptures, let us not travel, Lord, on the exterior road to them where they only speak against causes of sin; rather, hold us worthy of Your truth which lies within them and grant that we may continually, in a state of wonder, enquire into the reason for Your putting up with sinners. It is not because You wish to know something that You do not know that You provide time for sinners, waiting for a yes or no to repentance — to think such a thing, O Lord, of Your initial purpose is shocking, for it anticipates in its knowledge well before our being constituted with all the stirrings of our human nature. This would only be appropriate with human beings in this world, who do not know what will happen tomorrow.

87. (III.7.43) What is true and beautiful is this: that we should reflect on Your holy nature: the fact that You put up with a sinner is because of Your goodness and mercy beyond measure, even if You know that that person is not going to repent. You await the outcome, not as someone who has no knowledge of it, but You put up with them because of Your compassion, seeing that, being omniscient, all things are revealed to You. Your love towards humanity is immeasurable, O our Creator!

88. (III.7.44) O Lord, let not the goodness which You pour out over all be for me an excuse for evil and so, because of Your kindness, I make bold with evil actions. Hold me back with the reins of Your mercy so that I may be capable of withstanding the stirrings which assail me and the chance events that I meet with. Send Your holy angel as a guardian for us and heal the infirmity of my thoughts which, being mortal, I may have. Preserve my footsteps from the snares of the enemy which he has hidden against me, leading the way to the wickedness of sin.

89. (III.7.45) Above all, my God, preserve me from the folly of the intellect which imagines erroneous ideas, full of madness and worthy only of lamentation. It imagines such things in the presence of Your majesty with an abominable conception concerning its existence. Grant me, Lord, the humility which recognizes the limits of human nature and the wretchedness of its feeble state. Grant me a mind with upright knowledge, such as is appropriate for rational beings.

90. (III.7.46) O Guide of life, be revealed to me in my thoughts, and show me the paths leading to converse with You. Create in me, within myself, spiritual light which consists in the knowledge of Christ my Lord, so that, with that knowledge, I may discover Your reality and think sound thoughts concerning Your Godhead, and concerning matters of my soul. May I not, Lord, be tested at the hand of my adversary, resulting in derision from the demons for those who are tempted by pride and are handed over to them.

91. (III.7.47–8) Rather, lead me under the protection of humility as I grow in knowledge of You, strengthened by Your grace.

I venerate the great light of creation, Jesus Christ, who has shone out at His due time,[71] in accordance with the ineffable purpose of God, the creator of all—a purpose which He devised before all moments and times to send forth, to the honour and joy of creation, the only-begotten light, issuing from the Divine Nature. For He will have fulfilled His purpose in actual fact with the consummation of this world,[72] once He has shone out in our hearts and, at a time that pleases His will, has brought us close to His great purpose for the world, {48] and has returned me to the house of my Father,[73] and shown me the inheritance of glory which He has prepared for me beyond the limitation of the ages. Because of this He has brought me into the created world so that I might appear as a part of the creation of the Good One who has constituted everything in creation. Blessed for eternal ages is the honour it possesses! Amen.

---

[71] Cf. John 8:12; 2 Corinthians 4:6.
[72] Cf. Mattew 13:39; 2 Peter 1:19.
[73] Cf. Luke 15:17 (the Prodigal Son).

INDIVIDUAL PRAYERS

(a) Prayers from the First Collection[1]

92. (I, p. 209; Discourse 30)
For the time of 'unseen martyrdom' for solitaries in their fight against the evil of sin.

Our Lord, all-powerful, fountain-head of all assistance, at these times that are veritable times of martyrdom, give support to the souls which have joyfully betrothed themselves to You, the heavenly bridegroom, and with complete purity of emotions, and without guile, have given to You the solemn promise of a consecrated life: grant in them the strength to subdue the rebel powers and everything that has raised itself up in opposition to the consecrated life, so that these souls may not be disturbed from their set purpose as a result of unbearable constraint at the time when the great struggle against evil is being waged.

93. (I, p. 223; Discourse 34)
Prayer to know God in order to love Him.

Make me worthy to have a knowledge of You, Lord, in order that I may also love You. I do not ask for that knowledge

---

[1] The references are to the page and Discourse number in Bedjan's edition of the Syriac text; for correspondences with the Greek and the English translation by the Holy Transfiguration Monastery, see the Concordance at the end of this book.

which comes with fragmentation of the mind, as a result of the exercise of learning; rather, make me worthy of the kind of knowledge as a result of which the mind, as it gazes upon You, becomes filled with the praise of Your Divine Nature, seeing that its very act of gazing steals away from it all apperception of the world.

Make me worthy to be raised up, away from the gaze of the self-will that gives birth to fantasizing thoughts; rather, may I gaze upon You, being constrained by the bonds of the Cross, caught up in that second part of the process of the mind's crucifixion, where the role of its liberty is no longer occupied with the service of the emotions, thanks to that constant gaze upon You that lies beyond natural human ability.

Place in me the crucible of Your love, so that I may become crazed in love with You, far removed from the world.

Stir up within me an understanding of that humility of Yours which You displayed in this world by means of the bodily vestment in which You clothed Yourself, taken from our human limbs; and so, by constant and unfailing recollection of this I may accept with delight the low estate of my human nature.

94. (I, p. 224; Discourse 34)

If we do not make ourselves humble, O Lord, You will not cease humbling us.

95. (I, p. 278; Discourse 36)

O Lord, do not bring me into testing of this sort: even the strong and the experienced barely come out victorious.

96. (I, p. 279; Discourse 36)

In the face of temptation from the devil, following the example of the saints, entrust the battle into God's hands, saying:

You are the mighty one, and the battle belongs to You: fight, Lord, and be victorious in it on our behalf.

97. (I, p. 306; Discourse 40)

O Christ, who alone is mighty, how blessed is that person for whom You are their source of assistance, and in whose heart lie the steps that lead up to You. Turn our faces away from the world, O Lord, by means of a desire for You; in this way we shall see the world as it really is, and not take shadows for reality. Put in our minds, before we die, a sense of eagerness so that, at the time of our departure, we may be aware of the reason why we came into this world and are leaving it. In this way, as we seek to fulfil the task for which we were called, in accordance with Your original purpose in placing us in this life, we may have in our minds a confident hope of receiving the magnificent things which, according to the promises of Scripture, have been prepared by Your love at the second creation—the recollection of which are guarded by us in hidden faith.

98. (I, p. 346; Discourse 50)

Blessed is the person who has found You, O Haven of all joys!

99. (I, p. 359; Discourse 50)

Glory be to Your immeasurable grace! Now the flood-waters of Your grace have silenced me and I have not the ability left to stir, not even to give thanks to You! With what tongues can we thank You, O Good sovereign who has love for our lives?

Praise to You in both the worlds You have created—the one for our education, the other for our delight: praise to You from all those whom You have brought into existence in order to have a knowledge of Your glory, now and always ad for eternal ages, Amen.

100. (I, p. 431; Discourse 62)
Isaac explains that 'eternal life' means consolation in God.
O Lord, fill my heart with eternal life!

101. (I, p. 435; Discourse 62)
O Jesus Christ, sovereign of both worlds, make me worthy of a yearning for You!

102. (I, p. 435; Discourse 62)
O Lord, make me worthy to die in truth to involvement in this world.

103. (I, p. 436; Discourse 62)
O Lord, make me worthy to reject my own life for the sake of life in You.

104. (I, p. 442; Discourse 64)
May it be Your will in me to bring to completion in actual fact this good which I have chosen and desired to undertake if it accords with Your will. The willing of it is easy enough for me, but to carry it out, I am unable without a gift from You— though in reality both the willing and the carrying it out really belong to You, for it was not without Your grace that I assented to and was moved by it.

105. (I, p. 449–50; Discourse 65)

O Christ, the summation of truth, cause Your truth to shine out in our hearts, so that we may recognize how to walk in Your path in accordance with Your will.

106. (I, p. 453; Discourse 65)

Hold me worthy, Lord, to behold in my soul Your mercy before I depart from this world, so that, at that hour, I may be aware in myself of the comfort that has been experienced by those who have departed from this world with good hope.

Open up my heart, O my God, in Your grace and purify me from association with sin. Tread out in my heart the path of repentance, O my Lord and my God, my hope and pride, my strong refuge: in You may my eyes receive illumination, and may I have an understanding of Your reality, O Lord.

Hold me worthy, Lord, to taste the delight of the gift of repentance whereby the soul is kept apart from cooperating with sin and everything that is willed by flesh and blood.

Hold me worthy, Lord, to taste this suffering wherein is placed the gift of pure prayer. O my Saviour, may I attain to this wondrous crossing-point where the soul leaves the visible world and begins to experience the novel stirrings of entry into the spiritual world and new kinds of perception.

107. (I, p. 546; Discourse 80)

On arising for night vigils.

O my Lord and my God, who visits Your creation, before Whom are revealed our passions and the weakness of our human nature in the face of the strength of our adversary:

protect me from his wickedness, for his might is great while our human nature is wretched and our strength is weak. Therefore I beg You, O gentle Lord who are aware of our weakness and carry the burdens of our sick stare, preserve me from tumultuous thoughts and the violent onset of the passions. Hold me worthy of this holy mystery, so that I may not spoil its savour through my passions, and so be found presumptuous in Your presence. Rather, may I stand before You with chaste thoughts and with a luminous mind, as befits Your holiness, whose radiance cannot even be contained by the chariot of the seraphim who, in their delight, by means of their fiery movement, signify and utter cries of 'Holy' to Your being.

108. (I, p. 548; Discourse 80)
The prayer for forty years of 'one of the Fathers' (Apollo).
I have sinned, as a human being, on Your part as God, forgive me.

(b) Prayers from the Second Collection

109. (II.1.71) O Christ, the immense delight whose hope is far exalted above human thought, sow Your hope in my thoughts, so that by the perception of You, my mind may be released from gazing on earthly things. It is not possible, Lord for it to be released from distraction over earthly things except by being distracted by You; nor is it possible to see anyone as being bad, unless one is utterly alien to the knowledge of Your hope, having one's vision confined on the ground like a mole.

110. (II.1.72) Hold me worthy, Lord, to be dead to everything, and from this deadness may I be held worthy of the perception of the mystery of the New Life.

[Chapter III of the Second Collection consists of four sets of numbered Kephalaia, or Headings, on Spiritual Knowledge; the prayers nos. 111–122 come from the first three sets and are designated below as K.I–III].

111. (K.I.34) *Let the following prayer not cease from your heart, day or night:*
O Lord, save me from darkness of soul!

112. (K.I.81) O God, hold me worthy of the taste of delight that is situated in true repentance, and by which the truly penitent are daily nourished — people who do not despise weeping and mourning, or call it child's work: for they eat of the 'honeycomb' that is spoken of.[2]

113. (K.I.84) O Lord, who has brought me out of the world as far as the senses are concerned, by the might of Your holy right hand, hold me worthy to depart [from it] noetically with the stripping off of the stirrings of the corporeal world, so that I may follow You fully, nothing apart from You being seen by me, except the wandering about in the hiddenness of Your glorious mysteries. O Lord, cleanse my heart from meditating on earthly things, and direct my gaze towards that hope which is to come.

114. (K.I.86) O Only-begotten from the womb of the Father, the beauty of whose being puts the spiritual worlds in a [state of] wonder at every moment, out of love for mortals You covered

---

[2] 1 Samuel 14:27.

over Your glorious radiance with the veil of the flesh,[3] and You were manifested to the world under a lowly appearance, in Your grace hold me worthy, Lord, that I become forgetful of the world of time out of desire for You. May I not be mindful of the flesh, subject to corruption, in which I am held by the dominion of this dark world. Depict on my hidden mind, with the delineations of the Spirit, the mysteries of Your hiddenness; and may I delight in You in my hidden self at the stirrings which see without the physical eyes.

115. (K.I.88) O Christ, who died for us out of love for us, deaden sin and strip away from me that 'Old Man',[4] so that, with renewal of World'. O God, the heaven and the highest heavens do not contain You, [yet] You chose from us a rational temple[5] for Your dwelling place, hold me worthy to become a dwelling place for Your love—[a love] at the perception of which saints have forgotten themselves and become crazed [in following] after You, all the time mingled with You in the inebriated state of their love for You. They did not turn back again once they had drunk from this fresh spring [to meet] their thirst for Your love, for You had made them drunk with the wonder of Your mysteries.

116. (K.I.90) O hidden Mystery, who was revealed in our [human] body which had grown worn out, reveal in me the mystery of the renewal of the saints who receive in pledge already here [on earth] the assurance of the good things that are to come.

---

[3] Cf. Hebrews 10:20.

[4] Cf. Ephesians 4:22, Colossians 3:9. K.I.88 features in the *Shebitho*, or collection of weekly monastic prayers, for the Ninth Hour on Sundays.

[5] Cf. John 2:19.

In the stripping off of Your flesh You laid bare the [spiritual] rulers and authorities,[6] and clothed our human nature in the garment of incorruptibility. O Lord, strip off from me the [Old] Man subject to corruption in the mystery of the renovation, and cause the stirrings of the 'New Man' to burgeon in my hidden limbs: with whom at baptism You clothed me in symbol, and who, in the world to come, is given in reality, for the delight of all who cherish Your love, who have worn themselves out for Your sake here [on earth].

117. (K.II.8) Praise to the vastness of Your immeasurable love, praise to the wondrous nature of Your incomparable grace, praise to the inaccessibility of Your coming down to our level: You set the spiritual beings in a state of wonder that they could not explain. Finally, with the reality of their body, You raised them up to the contemplation of Your eternal thought concerning their establishment.

118. (K.II.30) O Christ, who gives life to all, it was for the setting aright of the human race that, hidden in Your divinity from the eyes of the seraphim, You appeared in a human body to the world, give me wisdom on the road to You, grant me the wisdom to know how to draw near to Your lordship. Cause hope in You to shine out in my heart so that I may become inebriated with it at every moment, and forget the mortal world at the pleasure of hope in You. O my God, hold me worthy of that forgetfulness which peers out at every moment over the saints as a result of the stirring of the hope in You.

---

[6] Cf. Colossians 2:15.

119. (K.II.58)

When you fall on your face before the Cross in prayer at the beginning of the Office, before you begin on the Office itself, request this from God and ask Him with pain from the heart that He should grant to you perseverance in it, so that, without feeling it irksome, you may be able to hold out in the recitation of the verses without having in you any battle with disturbance; [say]:

Grant to me, O Lord, luminous stirrings which gaze on You during this entire Office in the verses that issue from my mouth.

120. (K.II.81) *When you pray, say the following in your prayer:*

O merciful God, send to me from Your exalted sanctuary the gift of repentance by which I may approach You, the Lord. O God, open up my heart to become aware of what is beneficial for me—that acute awareness before which a neglectful mentality cannot stand, that awareness which casts confusion on the sense of tranquility in the passions.

121. (K.II.92) *Pray this in your solitary state continuously:*

O God, hold me worthy of this suffering of the life of mourning in my heart. O God, erase worldly converse from my heart.

122. (K.III.72) Praise to You, the One hidden from all and concealed in Your judgment, anterior in Your knowledge to all You have established, whose love is outpoured more than the sea: You have hung a curtain of difficulty over the face of Your kindness in order to restrain our propensity [to do wrong]. For if You had wanted to give us complete knowledge from the very beginning, You would not have placed us in this world, but [as it is] for the moment You have hidden those things which belong to Your nature, while things that do not belong to it, You are manifesting for [the sake of] the weakness of Your servants. These are things the precise nature of which

You have not granted even to those heavenly and exalted essences until their time dawns, in accordance with the boundary decided in Your intention, beyond [human] comprehension, for the revelation of their hidden character. In this expectation the invisible creation exists with groans concerning us,[7] so that when that hope comes out into the open, the knowledge of which it received at the incarnation of Christ; they will escape from any compulsion to waver while we will escape from the chastisements of the mortal condition.

123. (II.10.41) O Christ, Fountainhead of life, make me worthy to taste of You, so that my eyes may grow light;[8] O Compassion and mercy who have been sent to the world, O Hope of creation, cause me to taste of the delight of Your hope, so that I may be blind as far as the world is concerned, but illumined in spirit; and through Your love may my life become inebriated, so as to forget the world and its affairs.

May we be captivated and led to You through our minds, as we hold converse with Your great splendour. Do not let the world captivate us through harmful converse with it; rather, make us worthy to serve before You with attentiveness, in accordance with Your will; and may we praise You in an undisturbed way, in great peace, at all times.

Grant us, O Lord, a mouth filled with the praise of You, and a mind too which bears suffering. Make our understanding resplendent with a purity that cleanses the emotions, so that we may be an acceptable sacrifice[9] for You, and one without blemish, at all the times of our prayers.

---

[7] Cf. Romans 8:26.
[8] Cf. 1 Samuel 14:27.
[9] Philippians 4:18.

Cause Your hidden power to dwell in us, so that the senses of our souls may be strengthened, in order that our soul may mystically strike up a song filled with wonder. And thus may we sing praise at every moment along with the hallelujahs of the watchers on high in honour of the might of your being. As though in heaven, may we bear on our hidden limbs the sanctification of Your divinity. May we give thanks with all Your saints and worship Your great name without ever being sated, O Father, Son, and Holy Spirit, glorious in nature, for ages of ages, Amen.

124. (II.18.16) *There is no suffering more burning than the love of God.* O Lord, hold me worthy to taste of this fountain!

125. (II.18.18) Praise to Your grace, O God, praise to Your grace, O God. Praise to Your grace, O God who brought us into existence when we did not exist, granted us an unending being, providing us too with life, sense perception, reason, freewill and authority, five incomparably great gifts. For Your love did not just cause us to exist, but to be capable of reason, so that we might become aware of and enjoy the delight of intelligence and the pleasure of the vast gift of insight. And because it was not possible that we should be like You, without a beginning, You granted that we should be without an end, like You. Praise to You for the pleasure Your gift gives!

126. (II.20.24) As for me whose sores have turned foul and become putrid, please, O Lord, grant to me to take up the semblance of repentance in my soul, so that, as my hands are stretched out towards Your mercy, and as I sit at the door to grace, I may be held worthy of that hope which true penitents have received from You.

127. (II.20.25) Hold Your servant worthy, Lord, to scour away from his soul the mud of his actions by means of the tears of his eyes: by continually taking up Your help in the face of the infirmity of his thoughts, may he receive, through grace, an entry into Life, Amen.

128. (II.27.2) O God, grant me humility so that I may be freed from the lash, so that, with humility, I may draw near even to those delights of the mind of which I am unaware—however much I may desire to know them—before I acquire this humility.

129. (II.30.14) Lord, show me Your paths. And make known to me in spirit Your ways, so many and so ineffable; lead me on the course of truth and teach me the perfect knowledge of You which is to be found within the saints who have abandoned the world. O Christ, goal of the path of the saints, show me the path of truth in my heart, by means of the sweetness of reflection on You, so that I may travel and go on the path towards You until I see Your face.

(c) Prayers from the Third Collection

130. (III.2.9) O Christ, who enriches everyone, make firm in my soul the hope I have in You; bring me out of the darkness into an awareness of Your light, so that I may glorify You with the songs of praise that come from the heart, and not just the mouth.

131. (III.5.11) Praise to You, our Creator and Lord, for You have filled me with comfort and joy at the right contemplation of Your love. You have raised up my thinking from the depths of the earth and accepted it on the throne of Your very being, letting it wander about in the opulence of Your Divine Nature, in amazement at the ineffable mysteries of Your love, as it holds back from the multiplicity of creation in order to ascend to the place of its Maker.

Concordance for Prayers from the First Collection

The numbering of the Discourses in the First Collection varies according to the language and the edition. The following concordance will locate them in Bedjan's edition of the Syriac original, in the editions of the Greek by Pirard and Spetsieris, and in the English translation (from the Greek) published by the Holy Transfiguration Monastery in Brookline (HTM) (2nd edition).

SYRIAC Bedjan Discourse, page	GREEK Pirard Discourse: line	GREEK Spetsieris Discourse, page	English HTM Discourse, page
30, p. 209	20: 17–24	42, p. 174	32, p. 275
34, p. 223	26: 31–46	16, p. 58	36, p. 287
34, p. 224	26: 66–8	16, p. 59	36, p. 288
36, p. 278	28: 230–3	54, p. 215	39, p. 326
36, p. 279	28: 255–7	54, p. 216	39, p. 327
40, p. 306	32: 79–90	17, p. 63	43, p. 348
50, p. 346	41: 91	58, p. 236	51, p. 380
50, p. 359	41: 442–8	60, pp. 246–7	51, p. 389
62, p. 431	52: 52	38, p. 164	62, p. 439
62, p. 435	–	–	62, p. 441
62, p. 435	52: 111–12	38, p. 165	62, p. 441
62, p. 436	52: 132–3	38, p. 166	62, p. 442
64, p. 442	46: 22–8	59, p. 242	58, p. 426
65, p. 449–50	54: 92–4	34, p. 148	64, p. 452
65, p. 453	–	–	64, pp. 454–5
80, p. 546	66: 12–22	28, p, 120	75, p. 515
80, p. 548	66: 59–60	28, p. 122	75, p. 517

Main Editions and Translations

First Collection

A. Editions:

(1) Syriac:
Paul Bedjan, ed., *Mar Isaacus Ninivita, de perfectione religiosa* (Harrassowitz, 1909).

(2) Greek:
Editio princeps, ed. by Nikephoros Theotokis (Breitkopf, 1770); based on this is the edition by Ioakeim Spetsieris (Athens, 1895, with several reprints).

These old editions are now replaced by the excellent critical edition, based on the oldest manuscripts:

Marcel Pirard, *Abba Isaak tou Surou, Logoi Asketikoi* (Hiera Monē Ivērōn, 2010).

B. Translations:

(1) from Syriac:
Arent J. Wensinck, *Mystic Treatises by Isaac of Nineveh* (Koninklijke Akademie van Wetenschappen te Amsterdam, 1923).

Sabino Chialà, *Isacco di Ninive, Discorsi Ascetici: Prima Collezione* (Edizioni Qiqajon, 2021).

Discourses 1–6: Mary T. Hansbury, *St Isaac of Nineveh, On Ascetical Life*, Popular Patristics Series (St Vladimir's Seminary Press, 1989).

(2) from Greek:
Jacques Touraille, *Isaac le Syrien, Œuvres spirituels* (Desclée de Brouwer, 1981).

Dana Miller, ed., *The Ascetical Homilies of Saint Isaac the Syrian* (Holy Transfiguration Monastery, 1984; 2nd edn 2011).

Placide Deseille and Marcel Pirard, *Isaac le Syrien, Discours ascétiques* (Editions du Cerf, 2019).

Second Collection

A. Editions:

Chapters I–III:

Paulo Bettiolo and Valentina Duca, forthcoming.

Chapters IV–XLI:

Sebastian P. Brock, *Isaac of Nineveh (Isaac the Syrian, 'The Second Part', Chapters IV–XLI*, Corpus Scriptorum Christianorum Orientalium 554, Scriptores Syri 224 (Peeters, 1995).

B. Translations:

(1) Complete:

André Louf, *Isaac le Syrien, Œuvres spirituelles, II. 41 Discours récemment découverts*, Spiritualité orientale 81 (Abbaye de Bellefontaine, 2003).

Nestor Kavvadas, *Isaak tou Surou. Asketika*, Syriakē ekklēsiastikē grammateia 2, Tomos B, 1–3 (Thesbitēs, 2005).

Selja Seppälä, *Iisak Niniveäinen, Kootut teokset* (Valamon Luostari, 2005) [also includes the First Collection].

(2) Partial:

Chapters I–III:

Sebastian P. Brock, *Isaac of Nineveh, Headings on Spiritual Knowledge (The Second Part, chapters I–III)*, Popular Patristics Series (St Vladimir's Seminary Press, 2022).

Chapters IV–XLI:

Sebastian P. Brock, *Isaac of Nineveh (Isaac the Syrian), 'The Second Part', Chapters IV–XLI*, Corpus Scriptorum Christianorum Orientalium 555, Scriptores Syri 225 (Peeters, 1995).

Chapter III (Headings on Spiritual Knowledge):

Paulo Bettiolo, *Isacco di Ninive. Discorsi spirituali e alti opuscoli* (Edizioni Qiqajon, 1985) [also includes Chapters IV, V, XXXII, XXXV and XXXIX].

Manel Nin, *Isaac de Nínive, Centúries sobre el coneixement* (Editorial Pòrtic, 2005) [also includes Chapter V].

THIRD COLLECTION

A. Edition:

Sabino Chialà, *Isacco di Ninive. Terza Collezione*, Corpus Scriptorum Christianorum Orientalium 637, Scriptores Syri 246 (Peeters, 2011).

B. Translations:

Amdré Louf, *Isaac le Syrien, Œuvres spirituelles*, III, Spiritualité orientale 88 (Abbaye de Bellefontaine, 2009).

Sabino Chialà, *Isacco di Ninive. Terza Collezione*, Corpus Scriptorum Christianorum Orientalium 638, Scriptores Syri 247 (Peeters, 2011).

Mary T. Hansbury, *Isaac the Syrian's Spiritual Works* [Part III], Texts from Christian Late Antiquity (Gorgias Press, 2016) [with Syriac text].

ANTHOLOGY

Sabino Chialà, *Isacco di Ninive, Un'umile speranza* (Edizioni Qiqajon, 1999).

SHORT EXTRACTS

Donald M. Allchin, *The Heart of Compassion. Daily Readings with St Isaac the Syrian* (Darton, Longman & Todd, 1989).

Sebastian P. Brock, *The Wisdom of St Isaac the Syrian*, Fairacres Publications 128 (SLG Press, 1997).

Grigory Kessel, 'Isaac of Nineveh's Chapters on Knowledge', in M. Kozah *et al.*, eds., *An Anthology of Syriac Writers from Qatar in the Seventh Century*, Gorgias Eastern Christian Studies 39 (Gorgias Press, 2015), 253–80.

Further Reading

Hilarion Alfeyev, *The Spiritual World of Isaac the Syrian* (Cistercian Publications, 2000).

——, ed., *Saint Isaac the Syrian and his Spiritual Legacy* (St Vladimir's Seminary Press, 2015).

Valentina Duca, *'Exploring Finitude': Weakness and Integrity in Isaac of Nineveh* (Peeters, 2022).

Patrick Hagman, *The Asceticism of Isaac of Nineveh*, Oxford Early Christian Studies (Oxford University Press, 2010).

Andrew D. Mayes, *Diving for Pearls: Exploring the Depths of Prayer with Isaac the Syrian* (Liturgical Press, 2021).

Didier Rance, *Sur la route de la prière. Textes d'Isaac le Syrien* (Saint-Léger éditions, 2024).

Jason Scully, *Isaac of Nineveh's Ascetical Eschatology*, Oxford Early Christian Studies (Oxford University Press, 2017).

Valentin Vesa, *Knowledge and Experience in the Writings of St Isaac of Nineveh* (Gorgias Press, 2018).

INDEX OF BIBLICAL REFERENCES AND ALLUSIONS

References are to the prayer numbers in this edition

SLG PRESS PUBLICATIONS

FP1	*Prayer and the Life of Reconciliation*	Gilbert Shaw (1969)
FP2	*Aloneness Not Loneliness*	Mother Mary Clare SLG (1969)
FP4	*Intercession*	Mother Mary Clare SLG (1969)
FP8	*Prayer: Extracts from the Teaching of Fr Gilbert Shaw*	Gilbert Shaw (1973)
FP12	*Learning to Pray*	Mother Mary Clare SLG (1970)
FP15	*Death, the Gateway to Life*	Gilbert Shaw (1971, 3/2024)
FP16	*The Victory of the Cross*	Dumitru Stăniloae (1970, 3/2023)
FP26	*The Message of Saint Seraphim*	Irina Gorainov (1974)

FP28   *Julian of Norwich: Four Studies to Commemorate the Sixth Centenary of the Revelations of Divine Love*   Sister Benedicta Ward SLG, Sister Eileen Mary SLG, Sister Mary Paul SLG, A. M. Allchin (1973, 3/2022)

FP43	*The Power of the Name: The Jesus Prayer in Orthodox Spirituality*	Kallistos Ware (1974)

FP46   *Prayer and Contemplation* and *Distractions are for Healing*   Robert Llewelyn (1975, 2/2024)

FP48	*The Wisdom of the Desert Fathers*	trans. Sister Benedicta Ward SLG (1975)
FP50	*Letters of Saint Antony the Great*	trans. Derwas Chitty (1975, 2/2021)
FP54	*From Loneliness to Solitude*	Roland Walls (1976)
FP55	*Theology and Spirituality*	Andrew Louth (1976, rev. 1978, 3/2024)
FP61	*Kabir: The Way of Love and Paradox*	Sister Rosemary SLG (1977)
FP62	*Anselm of Canterbury: A Monastic Scholar*	Sister Benedicta Ward SLG (1973, 2/2024)

FP63   *Evelyn Underhill, Anglican Mystic: Two Centenary Essays*   A. M. Allchin, Bishop Michael Ramsey (1977, 2/1996)

FP67   *Mary and the Mystery of the Incarnation: An Essay on the Mother of God in the Theology of Karl Barth*   Andrew Louth (1977, 2/2024)

FP68	*Trinity and Incarnation in Anglican Tradition*	A. M. Allchin (1977, 2/2024)
FP70	*Facing Depression*	Gonville ffrench-Beytagh (1978, 2/2020)
FP71	*The Single Person*	Philip Welsh (1979)

FP72   *The Letters of Ammonas, Successor of St Antony*   trans. Derwas Chitty, introd. Sebastian Brock (1979, 2/2023)

FP74	*George Herbert, Priest and Poet*	Kenneth Mason (1980)

FP75   *A Study of Wisdom: Three Tracts by the Author of* The Cloud of Unknowing   trans. Clifton Wolters (1980)

FP81	*The Psalms: Prayer Book of the Bible* Dietrich Bonhoeffer,	trans. Sister Isabel SLG (1982)
FP82	*Prayer & Holiness: The Icon of Man Renewed in God* Dumitru Stăniloae (1982, rev. 2023)	

FP85   *Walter Hilton: Eight Chapters on Perfection & Angels' Song*   trans. Rosemary Dorward (1983, 2/2024)

FP88	*Creative Suffering*	Iulia de Beausobre (1989)

FP90   *Bringing Forth Christ: Five Feasts of the Child Jesus by St Bonaventure*   trans. Eric Doyle OFM (1984, 3/2024)

FP92	*Gentleness in John of the Cross*	Thomas Kane (1985)
FP94	*Saint Gregory Nazianzen: Selected Poems*	trans. John McGuckin (1986)

FP95   *The World of the Desert Fathers: Stories & Sayings from the Anonymous Series of the* Apophthegmata Patrum   trans. Columba Stewart OSB (1986, 2/2020)

www.slgpress.co.uk